# RED HOT CHILI PEPPERS
# FOR UKULELE

Photos by Steve Keros

ISBN 978-1-4950-7528-5

HAL•LEONARD®
7777 W. BLUEMOUND RD. P.O.BOX 13819 MILWAUKEE, WI 53213

In Australia Contact:
Hal Leonard Australia Pty. Ltd.
4 Lentara Court
Cheltenham, Victoria, 3192 Australia
Email: ausadmin@halleonard.com.au

Visit Hal Leonard Online at
www.halleonard.com

# The Adventures of Rain Dance Maggie

**Words and Music by Anthony Kiedis, Flea, Chad Smith and Josh Klinghoffer**

**Verse**

2. Tick tock, I want to rock _____ you like the eight - ies;
3. Rain Dance _ Mag - gie ad - vanc - es to the fi - nal;

cock block - in' is - n't al - lowed. _____
who knew that she had the goods? _____

Tug - boat Shei - la is in - to mem - 'ra - bil - ia;
Lit - tle did I know her bod - y was warm, _____ de - li - cious vi - nyl

who said three is a crowd? _ We bet - ter get it on the go.)
to your neck of the woods. _ I want to lick a lit - tle bit.)

**Chorus**

"Hey _____ now." _ We've got to make it rain some - how. _

_ She told me that you _____ would show me

5

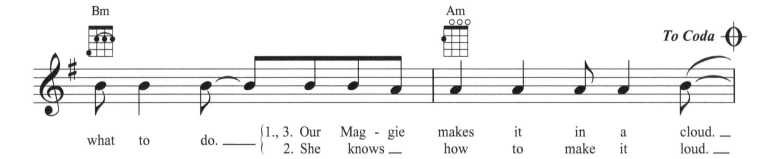

what to do. ___ {1., 3. Our Mag - gie makes it in a cloud. ___
2. She knows ___ how to make it loud. ___

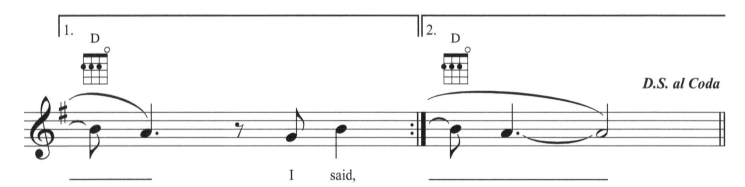

1.       D                                      2.    D

*D.S. al Coda*

___ I said, ___

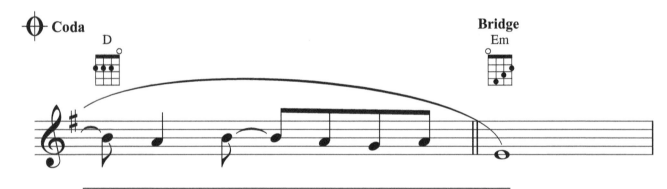

Coda     D                      **Bridge**
                                             Em

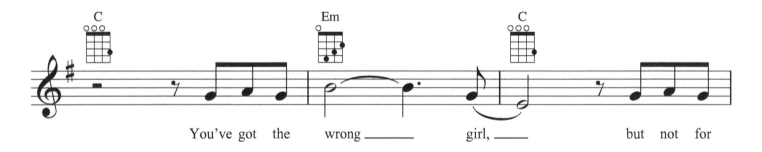

C                 Em             C

You've got the wrong ___ girl, ___ but not for

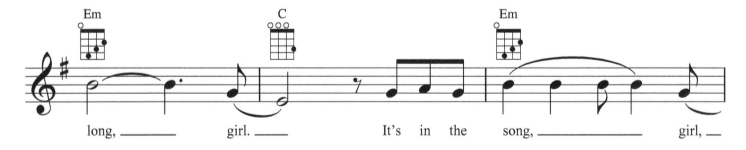

Em           C                       Em

long, ___ girl. ___ It's in the song, ___ girl, ___

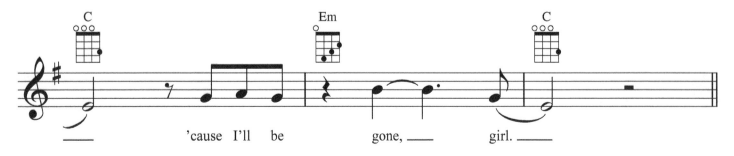

C                Em                 C

___ 'cause I'll be gone, ___ girl. ___

**Chorus**

"Hey _____ now." _____ We've got to make it rain some - how. _____
"Hey _____ now." _____ I want to rock this row - dy crowd. _____

_____ She told me that you _____ would show me
_____ She told me that you _____ would show me

what to do. _____ Our Mag - gie makes it in a cloud. _____ I said,
what to do. _____ She knows _ how to make it loud. _

**Outro**

_____ But not for

long, _____ girl. _____ It's in the song, _____ girl, _

_____ 'cause I'll be gone, bye bye bye, _ yeah. _____

# Breaking the Girl

**Words and Music by Anthony Kiedis, Flea, John Frusciante and Chad Smith**

We _____ were the two, _____ our lives _____ re - ar -
feel - ing no need _____ to make _____ me her

ranged. _____
home. _____

**Pre-Chorus**

Feel - ing so
I don't know

good _____ that day, _____
what, _____ when or why _____

a feel - ing of love _____ that day. _____
the twi - light of love _____ had ar - rived. _____

**Chorus**

Twist - ing and turn - ing, your feel - ings are burn - ing; you're break - ing the girl. _____

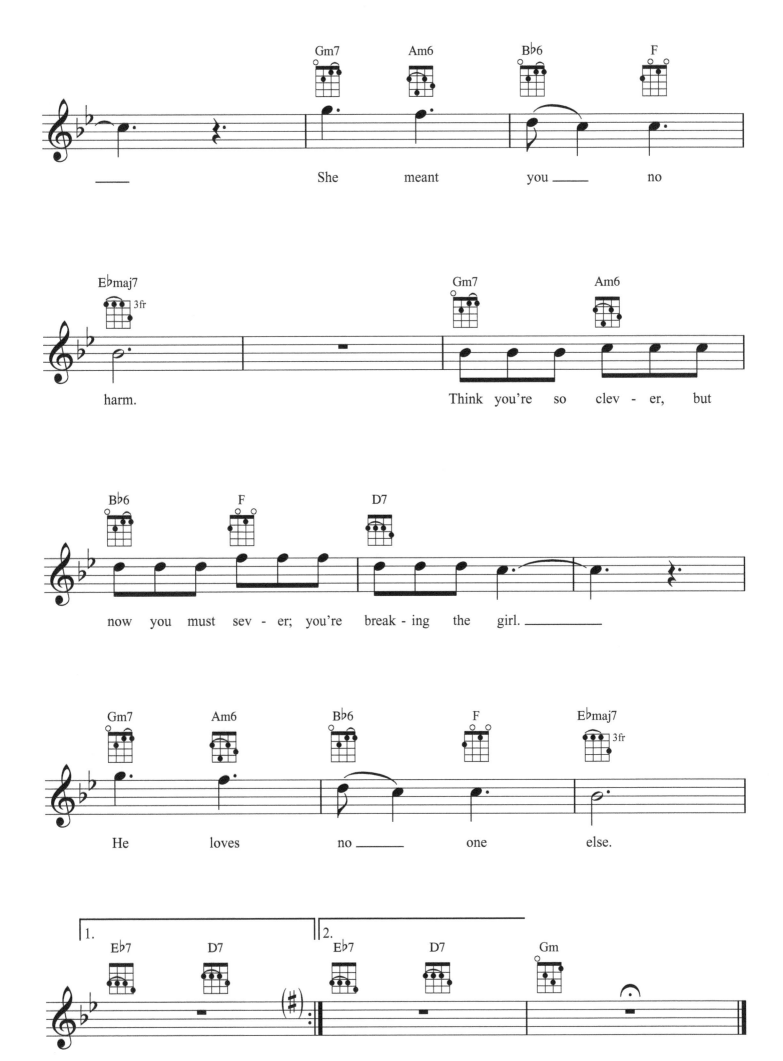

She    meant    you _____ no

harm.                 Think   you're   so   clev - er,   but

now   you   must   sev - er;   you're   break - ing   the   girl. _____

He      loves      no _____ one      else.

# Soul to Squeeze

from the Paramount Motion Picture THE CONEHEADS

**Words and Music by Anthony Kiedis, Flea, John Frusciante and Chad Smith**

With all the dy - ing trees _____ I scream. _____
It took a - way _____ my pain, _____ said please. _____
*Take me to the river, lay me on your shore. Well, I'll be comin' back, baby. I'll be comin' back for more.*

The an - gels in my dream _____
All let your ride be free. _____
*Vocal ad lib.*

had turned to de - mons of greed, _____ that's mean. _____
You got - ta let it be, _____ oh yeah. _____
*I cannot forget, but I will not endeavor. Simple pleasures are much better, but I won't regret it never.*

**Chorus**

Where I _____ go _____ I just don't know. _____ I got to, got to, got - ta

take it slow. _____ When I find _____ my peace of mind, _____

# Californication

**Words and Music by Anthony Kiedis, Flea, John Frusciante and Chad Smith**

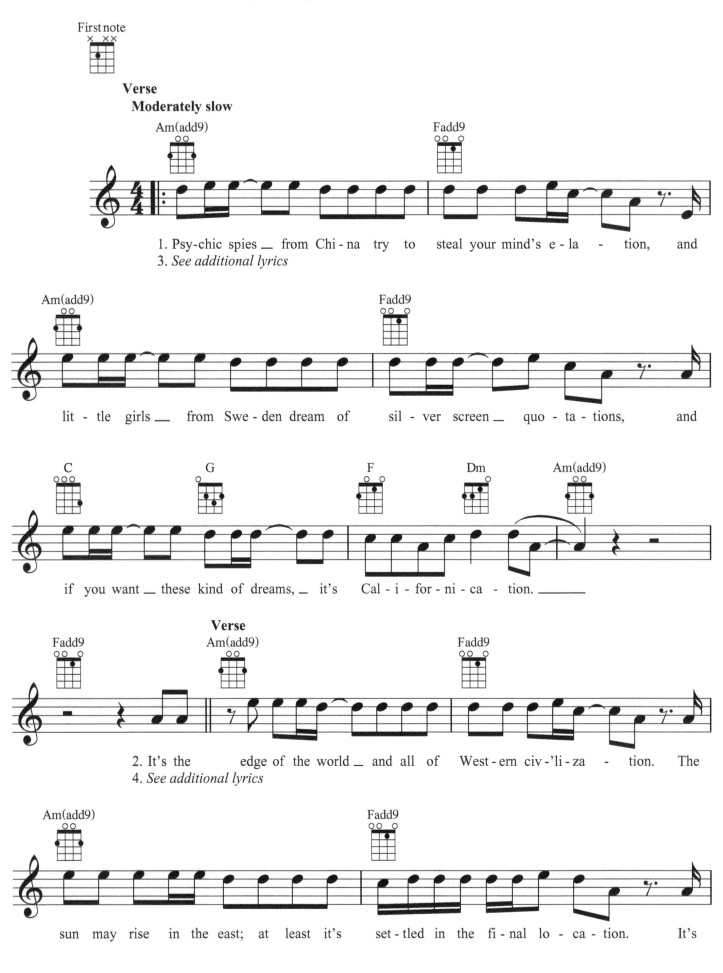

**First note**

**Verse**
**Moderately slow**

1. Psy-chic spies __ from Chi - na try to steal your mind's e - la - tion, and
3. *See additional lyrics*

lit - tle girls __ from Swe - den dream of sil - ver screen __ quo - ta - tions, and

if you want __ these kind of dreams, __ it's Cal - i - for - ni - ca - tion. _____

**Verse**

2. It's the edge of the world __ and all of West - ern civ -'li - za - tion. The
4. *See additional lyrics*

sun may rise in the east; at least it's set - tled in the fi - nal lo - ca - tion. It's

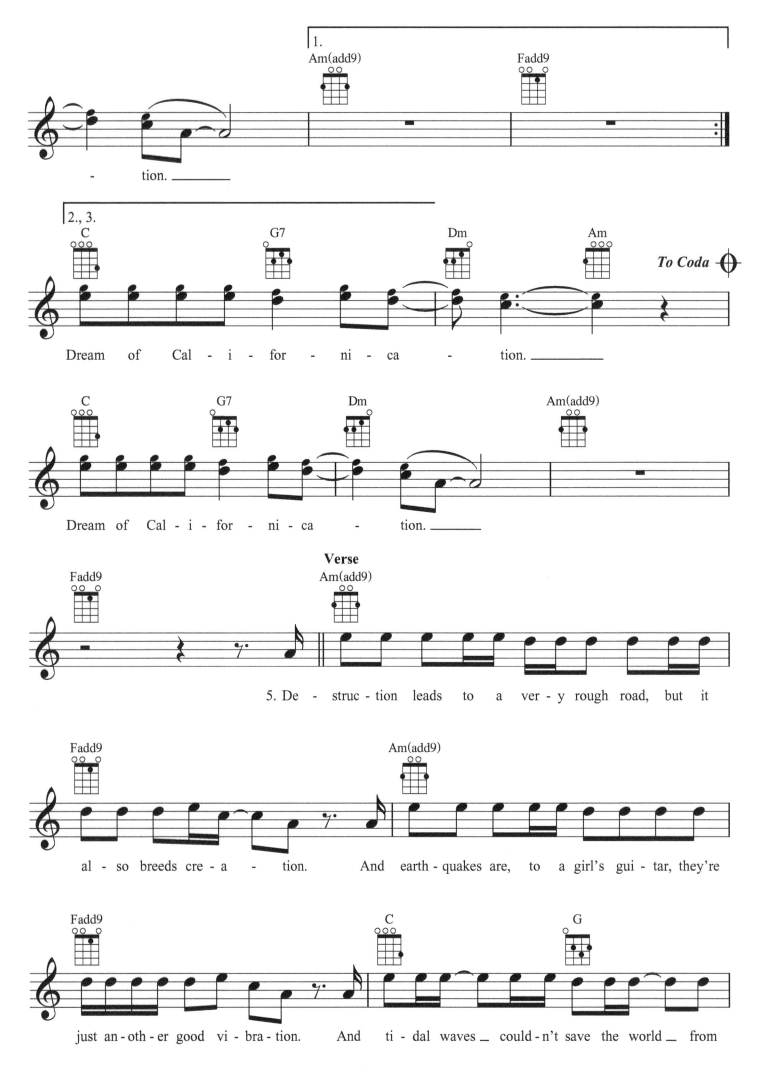

Cal - i - for - ni - ca - tion. ___ Oo. _____

**Pre-Chorus**

Pay your sur - geon ver - y well to break ___ the spell of ag - ing.

*D.S. al Coda*
*(take 2nd ending)*

Sick - er than the rest, there is ___ no test, but this ___ is what you're crav - ing.

**Coda**

Dream of Cal - i - for - ni - ca - tion. _____

*Additional Lyrics*

3. Marry me, girl.
   Be my fairy to the world; be my very own constellation.
   A teenage bride with a baby inside
   Getting high on information.
   And buy me a star on the boulevard.
   It's Californication.

4. Space may be the final frontier,
   But it's made in a Hollywood basement.
   And, Cobain, can you hear the spheres
   Singing songs off station to station?
   And Alderon's not far away;
   It's Californiaction.

   Born and raised by those who praise control of population.
   Everybody's been there, and I don't mean on vacation.
   First-born unicorn.
   Hard-core soft porn.

# Dani California

**Words and Music by Anthony Kiedis, Flea, John Frusciante and Chad Smith**

She nev-er knew that there was an - y-thing more ___ than poor.
Look-ing down the bar-rel of a hot met-al for - ty-five,
A lit-tle load-ed, she was steal-ing an-oth - er breath;

1.
What in the world does your com-pa-ny take ___ me for?

2., 3.
just an-oth - er way to sur - vive. _____
I love my ba - by to death. _____

**Chorus**
Cal - i-for - nia, rest ___ in peace. ___ Si - mul-ta -

- ne-ous ___ re - lease. ___ Cal - i - for - nia, show ___ your teeth. ___

___ She's ___ my priest - ess, I'm ___ your priest, ___ yeah, ___ yeah. ___

# Dark Necessities

**Words and Music by Anthony Kiedis, Flea, Chad Smith, Josh Klinghoffer and Brian Burton**

# My Friends

Words and Music by Anthony Kiedis, Flea, Chad Smith and David Navarro

# Otherside

**Words and Music by Anthony Kiedis, Flea, John Frusciante and Chad Smith**

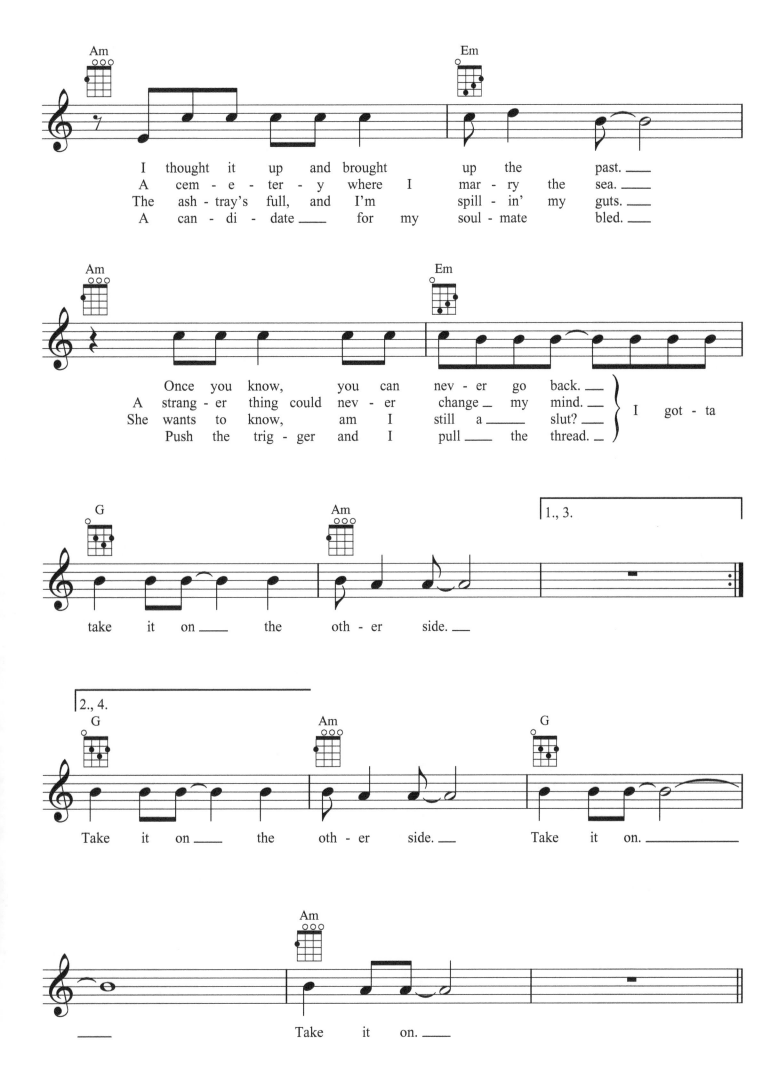

I thought it up and brought up the past. \_\_\_\_
A cem - e - ter - y where I mar - ry the sea. \_\_\_\_
The ash - tray's full, and I'm spill - in' my guts. \_\_\_\_
A can - di - date \_\_\_\_ for my soul - mate bled. \_\_\_\_

Once you know, you can nev - er go back. \_\_\_\_
A strang - er thing could nev - er change \_\_\_ my mind. \_\_\_
She wants to know, am I still a \_\_\_\_ slut? \_\_\_ } I got - ta
Push the trig - ger and I pull \_\_\_ the thread. \_\_\_

1., 3.

take it on \_\_\_ the oth - er side. \_\_\_

2., 4.

Take it on \_\_\_ the oth - er side. \_\_\_ Take it on. _____

\_\_\_ Take it on. \_\_\_

_____ me for a hard _____ ride. Burn me out, leave _____ me on the oth - er side. _____

I yell and tell it that it's not my friend. _____ I tear it

*D.S.S. al Coda 2*

down. I tear it down, and then it's born a - gain. _____

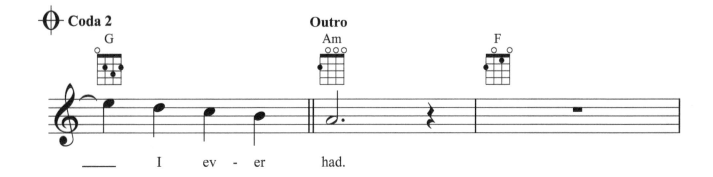

**Coda 2**   **Outro**

_____ I ev - er had.

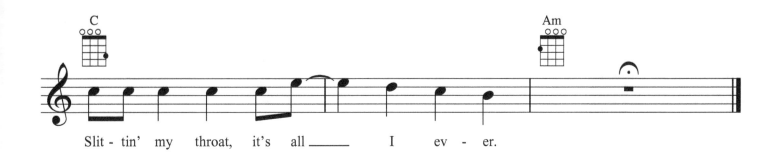

Slit - tin' my throat, it's all _____ I ev - er.

# Scar Tissue

**Words and Music by Anthony Kiedis, Flea, John Frusciante and Chad Smith**

young Ken - tuck - y girl in a push - up bra; ___
Step out - side, but not to brawl. And
sar - cas - tic Mis - ter Know - It - All. ___

fall - in' all o - ver my - self to lick your heart and taste your health.'Cause
au - tumn's sweet, we ___ call it fall. I'll make it to the moon if I have to crawl. And
Close your eyes and I'll kiss you 'cause ___ with the birds I'll share, _

**Chorus**

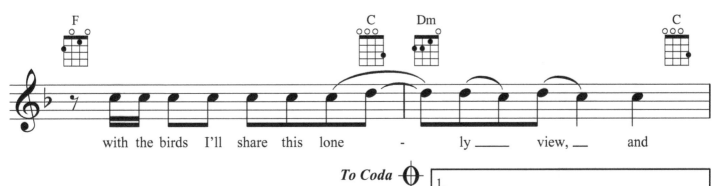

with the birds I'll share this lone - ly ___ view, ___ and

with the birds I'll share this lone - ly ___ view, ___ and

*To Coda*

1.

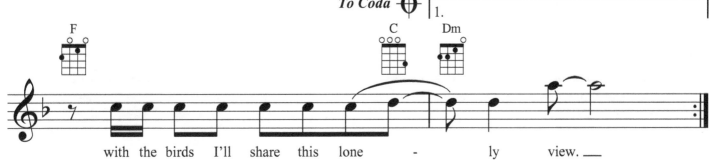

with the birds I'll share this lone - ly view. ___

2.

*D.S. al Coda*

- ly view. _

*Coda*

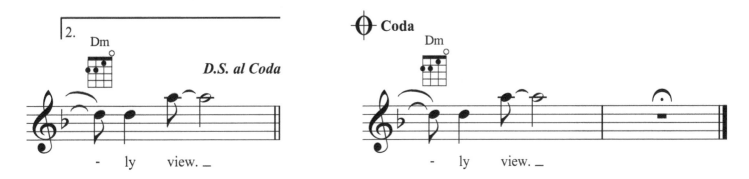

- ly view. _

33

# Show Me Your Soul

**from PRETTY WOMAN**

**Words and Music by Michael Balzary, Anthony Kiedis, John Frusciante and Chad Smith**

# Snow
## (Hey Oh)

**Words and Music by Anthony Kiedis, Flea, John Frusciante and Chad Smith**

1. Come to de - cide that the things that I tried were in my life just to get high on.
2., 3. *See additional lyrics*

When I sit a - lone come get a lit - tle known, but I need more than my - self this time.

Step from the road to the sea to the sky, and I do be - lieve that we re - ly on...

When I lay it on, come get to play it on all my life to sac - ri - fice.

**Chorus**

1. Hey, oh, ___ lis - ten what I say, ___ oh. ___
2., 3. *See additional lyrics*

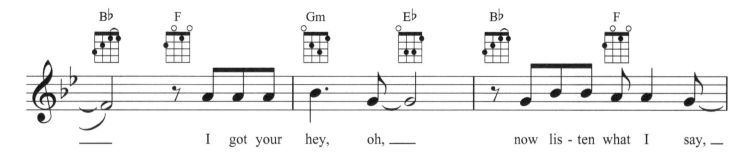

I got your hey, oh, \_\_\_\_ now lis-ten what I say, \_\_\_

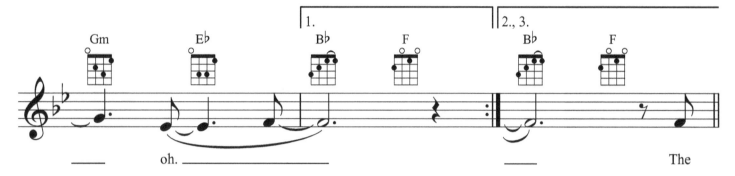

**1.** **2., 3.**

\_\_\_ oh. _____ \_\_\_ The

**Pre-Chorus**

more I see, the less \_\_ I know, the more \_\_\_ I like to let \_\_\_ it go.

Hey, _____ oh, whoa. _____

**𝄋 Chorus**

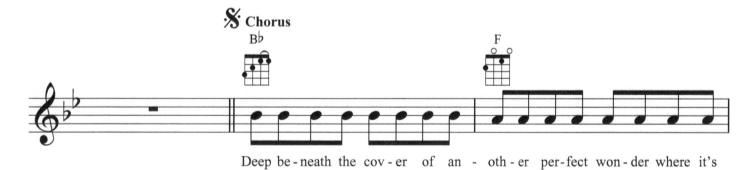

Deep be-neath the cov-er of an-oth-er per-fect won-der where it's

so \_\_ white as snow. \_\_ Pri-vate-ly di-vid-ed by a

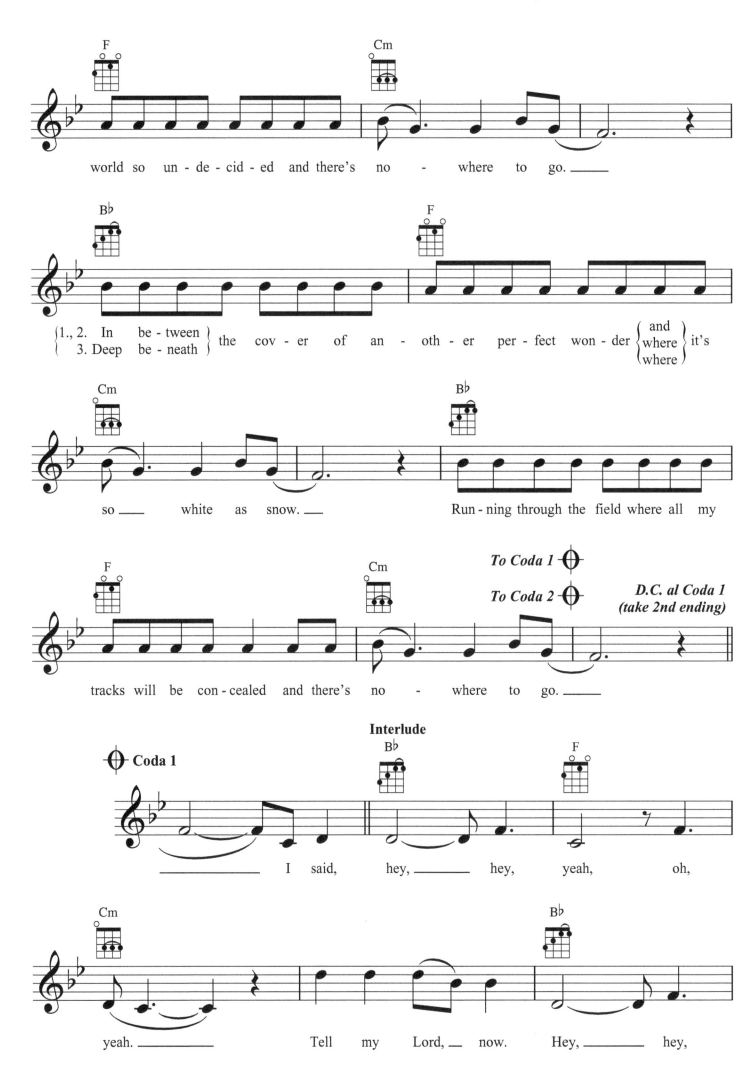

world so un-de-cid-ed and there's no - where to go. ___

(1., 2. In be - tween) the cov - er of an - oth - er per - fect won - der {and where where} it's
3. Deep be - neath

so ___ white as snow. ___ Run - ning through the field where all my

*To Coda 1* ⊕

*To Coda 2* ⊕

*D.C. al Coda 1 (take 2nd ending)*

tracks will be con - cealed and there's no - where to go. ___

**Interlude**

⊕ **Coda 1**

___ I said, hey, ___ hey, yeah, oh,

yeah. ___ Tell my Lord, __ now. Hey, ___ hey,

*D.S. al Coda 2*

**Additional Lyrics**

2. When will I know that I really can't go
   To the well once more? Time to decide on
   When it's killing me. When will I really see
   All that I need to look inside?
   Come to believe that I better not leave
   Before I get my chance to ride.
   When it's killing me, what do I really need,
   All that I need to look inside?

*Chorus 2:* Hey, oh,
   Listen what I say, oh.
   Come back and hey, oh.
   Look at what I say, oh, oh.

3. When to descend to amend for a friend
   All the channels that have broken down?
   Now you bring it up, I'm gonna ring it up
   Just to hear you sing it out.
   Step from the road to the sea to the sky,
   And I do believe what we rely on.
   When I lay it on, come get to play it on,
   All my life to sacrifice.

*Chorus 3:* Hey, oh,
   Listen what I say, oh.
   I got your hey, oh,
   Listen what I say, oh.

# Under the Bridge

**Words and Music by Anthony Kiedis, Flea, John Frusciante and Chad Smith**

1. Some-times I feel __ like I don't have a part - ner.
2., 3. *See additional lyrics*

Some-times I feel __ like my on - ly friend __ is the cit - y I live __ in, the

cit - y of an - gels. Lone - ly as I ____ am, to - geth - er we cry. __

2. I

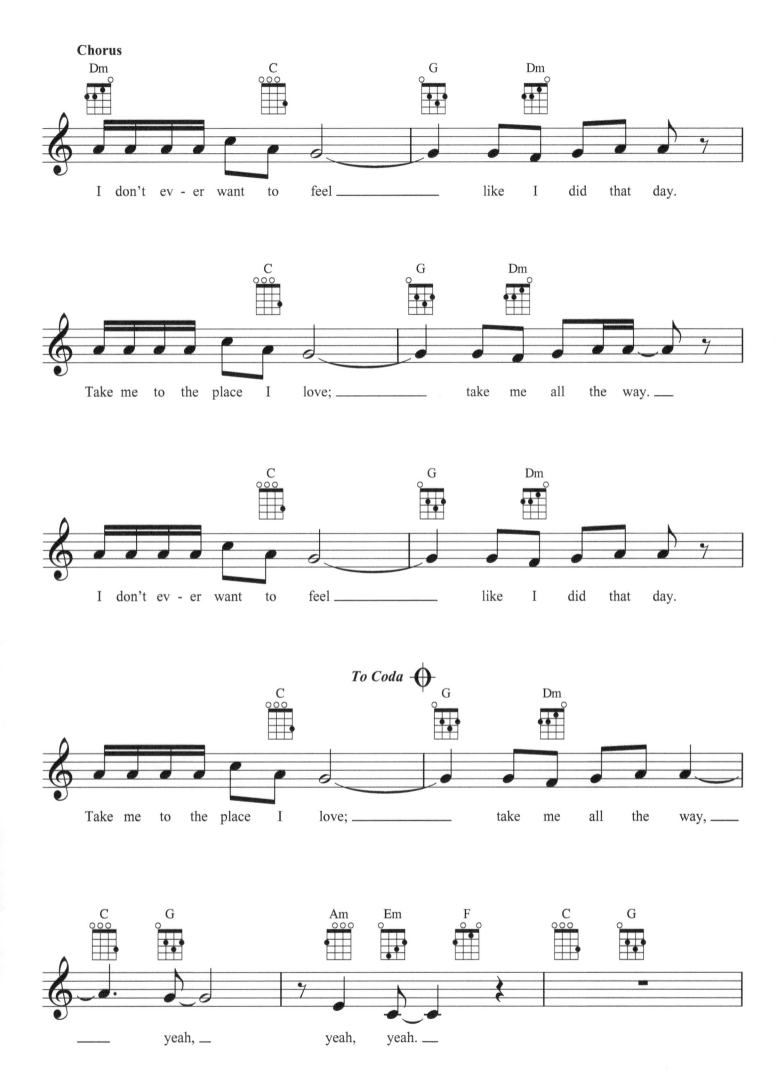

I could not get e-nough. __ Un-der the bridge __ down-town,

for-got a-bout my love. Un-der the bridge __ down-town,

I gave my life a-way. _____ *(Vocal 1st time only)*

*Additional Lyrics*

2. I drive on her streets 'cause she's my companion.
   I walk through her hills 'cause she knows who I am.
   She sees my good deeds and she kisses me windy.
   I never worry. Now, that is a lie.

3. It's hard to believe that there's nobody out there.
   It's hard to believe that I'm all alone.
   At least I have her love; the city, she loves me.
   Lonely as I am, together we cry.

# The Zephyr Song

### Words and Music by Anthony Kiedis, Flea, John Frusciante and Chad Smith

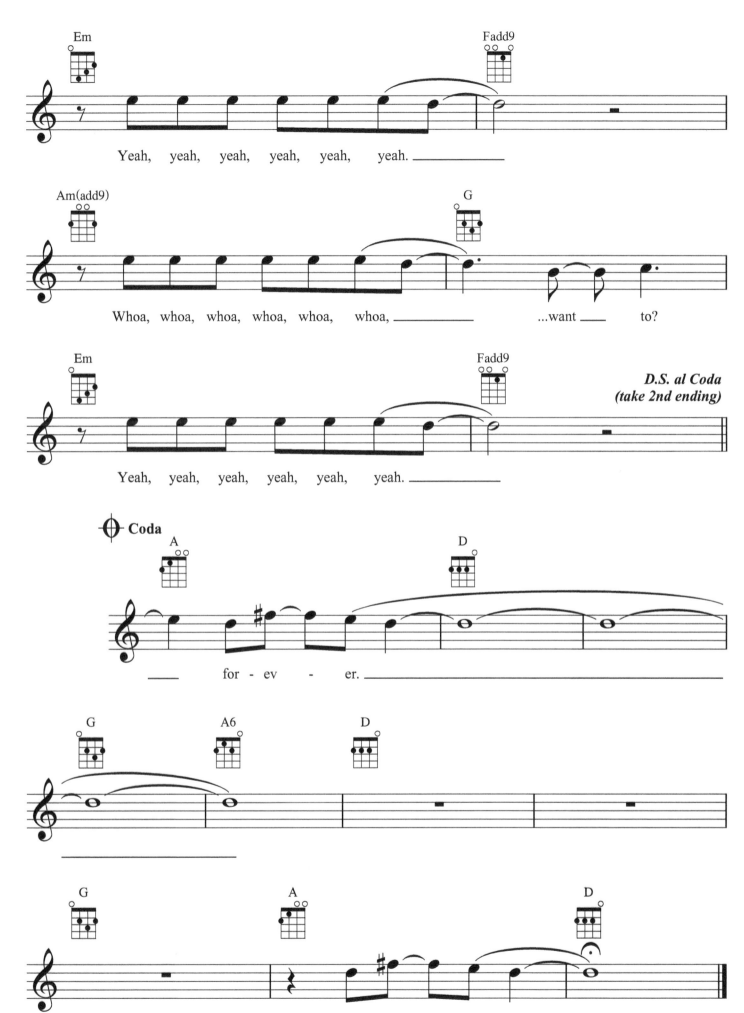

Yeah, yeah, yeah, yeah, yeah, yeah. _____

Whoa, whoa, whoa, whoa, whoa, whoa, _____ ...want ___ to?

*D.S. al Coda*
*(take 2nd ending)*

Yeah, yeah, yeah, yeah, yeah, yeah. _____

**Coda**

___ for - ev - er. _____

_____

For - ev - er. _____